The Song Shoots Out of My Mouth

The Song Shoots Out of My Mouth

by JAIME ADOFF

illustrated by Martin French

DUTTON CHILDREN'S BOOKS ■ NEW YORK

Text copyright © 2002 by Jaime Adoff
Illustrations copyright © 2002 by Martin French
All rights reserved.

CIP Data is available.

Published in the United States 2002 by Dutton Children's Books,
a division of Penguin Young Readers Group
345 Hudson Street, New York, New York 10014
www.penguin.com

Designed by Ellen M. Lucaire

Manufactured in China
First Edition
ISBN 0-525-46949-4
2 3 4 5 6 7 8 9 10

In loving memory of my mom:

Virginia Hamilton Adoff

A beautiful

Soul

An incredible

Mom

You will live forever in my heart . . .
J.A.

For Mr. Bear and the Little Peach
M.F.

Contents

The song shoots out of my mouth

Each word running fast across lips.
A direct line to my hips, twist and shake.
        My voice another arm, another leg.
        My throat the Cape Canaveral of my soul.
Song shuttle
                blasting off
                        into deep blue
        soprano sky.......
Why do
"I *still LOVE YOU*"
written on my palm,
fading now...
as cold front meets warm.
Pushing north from diaphragm to windpipe,
their first date my first pitch of life.
As the song:
SHOOTS
        Out of my mouth

        OUt of my doubt

        OUT of my self

        To you.......

9

I start the day with
my music buffet:
Morning fuel burns—cool jazz jams
on buttered toast.
    Hot salsa
    floats over
    everything I
    eat and drink
    in the
    song.
So much to choose from, can't pick
just one.
Fresh Squeezed Tina Turner—tastes so smooth.
Add a stack of Marvin Gaye—out the door to school.
Grab my James Brown bag lunch,
ready for my funk.
    Trade
my bologna for *your* Joni
Mitchell mashed.
Wash it down with a tall glass of
Beatle juice—stir with Ice Cube
Ahhhhh.....
    On the bus home,
the snack formerly known
as Twinkie is singing
its sweet cream melody
into my mouth.
    As the song:
booms and bumps
    and
grooves and funks
    and
rocks and rolls
    and
tastes so good.

The Drummer

I ride on cymbals crashing like metallic waves.
Oceans of colors in my ear.
Can't hear Mom 'cause I'm in love with my tom-toms.
Bass drum thunderclouds
roll beneath my feet.
I say "Hi,"
Hat
sssssssssssup
sssssssssssssup.
I'm cool
snap crack snare
lightning hits with more force
than a million recess bullies.
I serve Rack of Roto-Toms every day.
I practice till Mom yells, "Time to eat!"
Floor tom bows at my feet.
I play all night long.
In my sleep, I am
Moon
Bonham
Buddy
Blakey
10,000
Charlie
Watts
of
power
I am the drummer—
"What? OK, Mom, I'm coming!"

Mozart

explodes into my ears. Makes me drop my chocolate milk all over the cafeteria floor. I clean while the strings sing the melody. Pass it back—the orchestra plays catch.

I feel like an astronaut going to the moon. Just to refuel on my way to Mars. Then—Jupiter Symphony No. 41—playin' soccer on the sun, barefoot.

Goose bumps, football fields long. His sound surrounds me, and this table and this school.

Mozart's sooooo cool. Every song a hit.

What would it be like to talk to him?

What would I say?

Someday I wanna play like that. Write like that. Make sounds that sound like that.

But

Don't wanna end up like that.

The bell rings.

I put Mozart in my backpack. I can still hear him as I walk into class.

Concerto in C, Movement 3—Rondo on my mind. Hit my rewind.

Wonder if he was alive, would he stage dive?

I bet he would.

Mozart
explodes into my ears.
Makes me drop my chocolate milk,
all
over
the cafeteria floor.

down the street
Hip Hop
Loud Talk
Baggy shorts
past our knees.....

I'm MC Free: gonna be what I want,
no one can touch me, don't even try to front.
My rap is so hype, I can scribble or type.
My rhymes so smooth, make your booty wanna move.
After class kickin' back, do my math really fast.
Adding all the millions from my first single.
On the couch filet mignon and Pringles.
After Mom and taxes
I'll relax with
my fortune and fame.
I'll stay the same won't change at all.
Got 3 mansions with platinum walls.
I'm number one twice in every country,
first class, now
Delta won't bump me.
Private jet coast to coast, MC Free on your toast.
I'm the host with the most,
'Bout to blow
UP!!!

I'm all that, just wait and see....
we walk sideways
down the street.

Watch out.......

Diva

She is the
undisputed Queen of everything. Her walk says it all.
She's earned every note, every ounce of gold, and platinum
albums sold.
So many number-one songs, not enough fingers, toes, and thumbs
to count them all.
Her grace walks onstage before she does.
We wait, anticipate. Wonder from this side
what it would be like to be her. To be up there looking at us.
What does she think about?
The place goes dark. The storm before the calm.
Then without warning:
THE SONG
flows
out of her mouth.
Like a waterfall in slow motion.
A magic potion
poured slow and easy on the ears.
Then, just when you think it's safe to sit, the riffs come raining down.
On my head, no soul umbrella, instead I let the song soak, deep and long. Filling me
up with everything she has, everything she's lived, everything she is.
Her voice brings me close to tears.
I sing along and move, she is *all* about the groove.
I watch, as each note shakes hands with every fan.
Thanking
loving
kissing
hugging.
What's hers
is mine, is ours.
Her power
is
her voice
is
her soul
singing
to me
in this seat.

She is the
Diva.

My trumpet

sits in the corner of the band room.

It doesn't know that tomorrow it will be mine.

My first instrument. Ever.

I have a space on my shelf already cleared off.

I have *Trumpet for Beginners, One and Two.*

Been practicing on my sister's kazoo.

Already know the theme to *Rocky.* I'm gonna be so cool. I'll play with my back
to the audience like Miles Davis. Or twirl my trumpet around like they do on
MTV. I'll just have to wait and see. I know Mr. Cooper's gonna pick me.
He has to. He has to.

   After lunch: "The time has come," Mr. Cooper says.

I wait to hear my name:

".......Randolph, Bassoon"

"Taylor, Trombone"

"Higgins, Trumpet"

"*Myers,* Tuba"

   Tuba? No way!

It has to be a mistake. I can't play that thing. It's too big. Everyone's gonna laugh at me.

There's no Tubas on MTV.

Now I'll never be a star!

   "Hey, Higgins, I'll trade you instruments for a peanut butter sandwich.......

..... I'll even throw in my chips...... OK, a candy bar too......."

how i look
when i meet
michelle
at the
movies..........

A   lan

B   QUIET!

C   I told you so

D   on't tell Mr. Ryan I dropped his Stradivarius on the gym floor.

E   mail me when you get to Siberia.........

Practice makes _____?

Cats scratching
broken blackboards while
a thousand squeaky seesaws
tease rusty swing sets.
My "Lightly Row" sinks the boat.
Every dog on the block
runs away.
Birds drop from the sky.
CIA
and
FBI
have me on their most-wanted lists.
I practice, but never get better.
My brother says I should forget it.
Mom and Dad say they like how I play
as they get in their car and drive far away.
Mr. Jones, who wears earplugs,
tells me I sound good. I know that's a lie,
but still
I
Practice,
Practice,
Practice,
all the way to Carnegie Hall......
Or
at least to my first recital next Tuesday at Ms. Baxter's house.

Radio waves
     to my ears
     tickling the inside of my brain.
Every song, 3 and ½ minutes of fame.
     I'm in the song, in the band.
Pump my fist, raise my hand.
36,000 screaming fans yell:
                    HAROLD!
H A I R !   O L D!
H A I R !   O L D!
          SOLDOUT!
AGAIN!
Do the splits, then a three-sixty off my bed,
thrash my head to the beat.
Do a flying leap off my desk.
Make my best Rock n Roll face
as I play my tennis racquet guitar.
Upside down,
I play with my teeth/play with my feet.
Through the legs/ behind my back.
Rocking so hard, hit my head on the floor,
Hey, I'm OK.
Time for the—
          ENCORE:
          one more:
          Jagger
          Swagger
          Elvis
          twist.
I break out into a
          Keith
          Sweat
dripping down my neck.
I know I make the ladies weak in the knees
(whatever that means).
Song is fading......
Homework's waiting.
End of show.
H A I R !   O L D!
          has left the building.

Half/time

Our time to shine.
> Stepping perfectly n sync.
> *My trumpet spins*. Knees up to chin.
Notes in my head go express to fingertips.
STEP left
> *Sax around neck*, playin' *my* show.
Turn 360 and blow.
Head up high, Baritone to the sky....
STEP right
> *This drum's weighing me down.*
Straps digging in—Can't think about it now....
Twirl sticks—then hit—
lean back. Head up. My favorite part.
Hit-turn-twirl-spin—
Straps still diggin' in....
STEP left
> *I have the best instrument.* Got the power in my lips.
Make this Lion roar.
Love this move, so coool—little dance and shake—
we call it the TUBA QUAKE.
STEP right.
> *Trombone by my side*, pick it up
and slide to my solo, uh oh, I'm behind. Gotta catch up—Bye...
STEP left.
> *Sun beating on my big hat.* Head burning, Hot.
Baton in the air. Oops.
Lost it for a second in the clouds.
Flash of pride coming down, fast. Spin, once, twice, *s p l   i t s.*
Catch.
Sun still beating on my big hat.
Everyone stands and yells and screams......
We are the marching blue and green
We are the marching blue and green.....

"Go Lions!"

Half/time
our time to shine.

Fingers fly over black and white keys
My bi-racial melody plays on.
After class, all day long,
there will be permanent piano integration.
In school they teach the struggle,

       now

       and

       then

like these minor scales
a Major pain in my hands.

       But

I will overcome
we shall overcome.

       88 keys marching on,
past attack dogs and fire hoses.
Blue notes rise above martyred souls.

       All the wrongs become right,
as I shut my eyes tight.

       I am sharp, flat, white key and black.
Floating above my hands—in this trance.
Watching the song shoot out of my fingers, fly over black and white keys,
blackandwhitekeysblackandwhiteandblackandwhiteandblackwhiteblackwhiteblacwhitbla...........

You have exactly
one measure's rest
before you have to sing
a solo in front of the whole school.
You sang it perfectly in rehearsal.
Now your mind is blank.
Susie, who you've had a crush on since the 4th grade, is in the front row.
Katie, who you've had a crush on since the 5th grade, is in the second row.
You've just ripped your pants,
you're sweating buckets,
and
your shoes are untied.

Good luck.....

Reggae Snowday

"No schoo ta day Mon"
I wake to the sound
of my favorite DJ. Hear him say
the name of my school:
P.S. One-Twenty-Two.
"Cool runnings ta day"
kick back wita litt'l Bob MAAAAHLEEEE......
My mind plows into a ZIGGY snowdrift.
Throw reggae Snow Ball from highest Jimmy Cliff.
Watch it fall on silent Island road.
Explodes on hot sand
stuck between my toes.
Yah Mon
Reggae Snow is warm Ta Day.
My School Bus is stuck in the ten-foot waves.
I surf over to the blackboard. Do my book report on my back.
I'm relaxed. Sun Soaks into my white skin,
turns golden french fry brown.
No one around for miles, on this deserted Isle.
Just me and Mr. MAAAAAAAHLEEEEEE......
His voice Satisfies my soul
all reggae snowday long......

"My mistake Mon. All you dudes in P.S. One-Twenty-Two.
You gotta go to schoo. Now turn off the MAAAAAHLEEEEEE and catch your bus.
No snowday for you.
You're outta luck."

We play fast, hard
everything on ten—
"HOLD UP.
Tom, what chord is that man,
sounds like a chicken's dying!"
"Ben, you can't even play guitar.
I know what I'm doin'. Just stick
to screamin'—I mean singin'."
Dan's garage our Madison Square Garden.
      Old Christmas lights shine bright on my face.
I sing with almost teen hate and love,
"Hey Beth, drums are too loud, I can't hear myself sing!"
"Hey Ben, don't worry, you're not missin' much."
"What?"
 "Nothin'."
Low-slung guitar around neck.
     Not Generation X or Why?
the new sound
the next big thing.
"Can we have some bass here? Dan, are you even plugged in?"
"Oh my fault, my cable came out. OK, I'm plugged in again."
"You know what, just play with the cable out. I think you sound better that way."
"Shut up, Ben, you couldn't carry a tune if your life depended on it."
"Dan, you can be replaced, don't forget that."
"Oh yeah? You can't replace me, I'm the one who's got the garage, remember. And the amps and the drums and...."
"Oh shut up, Dan."
"You shut up, Tom."
"All of you shut up."
"Man, I quit."
"You can't quit, Ben, 'cause we're kicking you out."
"Too late, I quit first. Later."
"I quit, too. You guys suck."
"I'm outta here."
"Me too."
    This is our dream
running through our veins.
    Music is Everything.

    WE ARE
    JUNK YARD!!!!!!

Jazz Bath

Be Bop bubbles go
up my nose as I blow into my horn.
Pass the soap and the eighth notes, drip
into my eyes.
No more tears
no more fears.
My sax speaks for me. Says what I can't say. Which is a lot
these days. Now, teenage.
I trade 4's and 8's with Bird and Trane.
Outside my bathroom door,
I hear the roar of the crowd,
the roar of the crowd!
The roar of my sister screaming,
"GET OUT!!"

Percussion snail

Last row.
Orchestra.
5th period.
Locked in this jail
Too many bars
I'm the percussion snail.
Hurryup and w a i t
One hundred and eight, two, three, four....
Countdown to lunch.
2 more measures
and I'm on.
NOW!
I stand and play,
RAT, TAT, RAT-TAT-TAT;
OVER.

That's it?
I sit.
Locked in this jail
Too many bars
I'm the percussion snail.

according to me.
This is my music my church
my joy.
My hurt runs away
up to the second tier, the second tear
streaks down my cheek as her otherworldly voice sings.
Straight from heaven to me in this pew. My book opens to the page.
I can no longer hate, no longer wait for the next gospel to play.
I am free to float up high to the pipe organ.
Foot pedals marching to the Word. I   float   over   to my   house   looking
down   watching   Granny   dance   to   Ma

halia.

This   beautiful   gospel   day,

me   and   Ce Ce   sip   sweet   lemonade

under Mighty
                    Clouds of
                                        Joy.

          Aretha's   *Amazing*   Grace   plays   in   the

background   to   my   hopscotch.   Double   Dutch   with   the

Lord   and   my   best   friend   Denise.

We sing   as we   jump
and we   jump as   we sing

This   is   the   gospel

                    according

                    to me.

out of taped fingertips,
hard hands hit tougher skin.
Worn from years of getting beat, making beats fly through the air.
Two congas between legs, two more on the side. Now four, wait, he grabs one more. Five congas at one time. His hands no longer from man. Now just in the middle of the 1 and the and of 4, somewhere between Cuba and Baltimore. He smacks, flicks, hits, kisses, wishes he was faster. *"Used to be faster than this,"* he says. WOW! His wrists double-jointed, every finger broken at least once, that bump on his elbow makes another cool sound. He looks around the gym. All us kids wish we were him. We start playing the bleachers, call and response.
He stops to announce the next piece.
"Gasoline rhythms in an ocean of Latin Fire."
Man this is way better than choir.

Otra vez:
Flames shoot out of taped fingertips,
hard hands hit tougher skin.
Worn from years of getting beat s fly through the air,
beats
        fly
              through   the   air

beats

        fly

               through

                    the

                        air......

Way 2b

how this soda pop
tastes after mom
left it out
on the counter,
all night,
with the cap
off......

Coloratura
Soprano-singing in the stratosphere.
Long red gown flows to her shoes.
Curly hair doesn't even move as notes catapult from her mouth to waiting ears.
Her voice spans centuries as she glides across the stage, singing of Love and Hate and
Madness. In a flash she falls to her knees—Voice flying on Verdi wings—
breaking through Puccini clouds—carefully now, she weaves and twists her way—holding notes
letting them go, painting with colors, brush strokes of soprano soul.
She *is* the moment.
This moment that lasts a lifetime—of lessons and scales and tears and......
Now you don't even see her sweat.
She is
Coloratura
Soprano-singing in the stratosphere.........

Ba DA da da DA.
Got a brand-new guitar.
Ba DA da da DA.
Just the other day.
Ba DA da da DA.
Played it for five minutes.
Ba DA da da DA.
Then my mom took it away.
Ba DA da da DA.

See she got real mad.
Ba DA da da DA.
Said I couldn't go out.
Ba DA da da DA.
Got an F on my math test.
Ba DA da da DA.
Make me wanna scream and shout.....

I got the no guitar blues,
Can't play it no more.
It just sits in the corner
lookin' so bored.

I can't be with my friends,
can't play at the dance.
Me and my Algebra book
and my new leather pants.
My new leather pants.
my new leather pants.........

I got the no guitar blues,
rEEEEEEEEEEEEEEEEEEEEEEEEEEEEEEEE
AAAAAAAAAAAAL
BAAAAAAAAAAAAAAAAAAAAAAAAAAAD!!!!!!!!!

Which came first
speech or the song?
Village to village
Drums saying it all......
Very *l o n g*
distance calls.
Human cell phones
connecting the
present to the past.
Today with tomorrow
in your school, in my class.
Sitting in this chair, I learn history.
What, where, when. The song is more than music
It's who I am.
Him, her, me, you, we're all cut from
the same groove.
The same beats—same notes
might sound different to you
but in between the rests...
we are one, and two and three and four and
much much more.
Much much more, than that.
BUT
Now
back
to
the
song:
SHOOTS
Out of my mouth
OUt of my doubt
OUT of my self
for you
to breathe
for you
to be
the song
breathe
the song
deep into
your lungs
and
pass it on.....

Backnotes

MUSICAL TERMS & DESCRIPTIONS:

 # Sharp: Term used to describe a musical note or tone one-half step higher than the note named. This is indicated by the sign #. For example, the note C one-half step higher would become the note C#. The # sign raises the pitch of a note in any piece of music by one-half step.

***b* Flat:** Term used to describe a musical note or tone one-half step lower than the note named. This is indicated by the sign *b*. For example, the note A one-half step lower would become A*b*. The *b* sign lowers the pitch of a note in any piece of music by one-half step.

Measure: A group of beats (units of musical time), the first of which is usually accented. These groups can contain two, three, four, or more beats. They recur consistently throughout a composition and are marked off from one another by bar lines. A measure is also called a bar.

Trading 4's and 8's: In small jazz groups (and sometimes in big-band jazz) musicians may take turns at playing four- or eight-bar solo phrases. For example, a saxophonist may play a solo for four bars, followed by a trumpeter playing a solo for four bars. These "trades" usually happen after the longer solos and before the return of the theme (main melody) of the tune.

Coloratura Soprano: The highest voice type in classical singing. Coloratura sopranos can move their voices quickly through musical passages, singing fast and high with much ease.

ARTISTS & SUGGESTED LISTENING:

Keith Moon, 1946-1978 ("The drummer")
Legendary drummer for the rock group The Who. A brilliant but unpredictable drummer, Moon had an unconventional style that mirrored his "wild" personality. Arms flailing in a rhythmic tornado, Moon's inescapable talent greatly enhanced the best of The Who's music. Suggested listening: "The Ox" (1965) from *The Who Sings "My Generation"* and "Won't Get Fooled Again" (1971) from *Who's Next.* A greatest hits compilation CD from The Who is a good introduction.

John Henry Bonham, 1948-1980 ("The drummer")
The author's hands-down favorite rock drummer. Bonham was the driving force behind the famed rock group Led Zeppelin from the late 60s until his death in 1980. Bonham's style was a brilliant combination of power and finesse. With a heavy foot that could produce rapid-fire beats and hands that seemed to float over his drums and cymbals, Bonham's playing was an integral part of every Zeppelin song. Often imitated but never duplicated, John Bonham is probably the most influential rock drummer of all time. Suggested listening: "Bonzo's Montreux" from the CD *Coda* and everything ever recorded by Led Zeppelin.

Bernard "Buddy" Rich, 1917-1987 ("The drummer")
Buddy Rich took big-band drumming to another level, combining endurance, phenomenal dexterity, and amazing speed. Playing with remarkable technical precision and light-as-a-feather sensitivity, this drumming genius, who claimed he never practiced, amazed audiences. It is safe to say Buddy Rich greatly influenced just about anyone who ever picked up a pair of drumsticks. Suggested listening: *Buddy Rich vs. Max Roach* (1959, Mercury Records), *Swingin' New Big Band* (1966, Pacific Jazz), *West Side Story and Other Delights,* and *Krupa & Rich.*

Art Blakey, 1919-1990 ("The drummer")
Known as one of the greatest bandleaders and musicians in the history of jazz. He, along with Max Roach, established the drums as a truly musical instrument. With amazing skill, Blakey led his critically acclaimed group, the Jazz Messengers, for 36 years. Using complex rhythms and his signature press rolls, Blakey would drive a tune, steering it with a creative brilliance that has yet to be matched. Suggested listening: *At the Café Bohemia, A Night in Tunisia, Mosaic,* and *Free for All* (Blue Note Records).

Charlie Watts, b.1941 ("The drummer")
Has played with the Rolling Stones since 1963. His "less is more" groove-style playing perfectly complements the master of groove guitar, Keith Richards. Since the mid-1980s, Watts has also pursued a career as a jazz drummer. In 1991 Watts formed the Charlie Watts Quintet, and in 2000 formed the Charlie Watts/Jim Keltner

Project. Suggested listening: *Beggars Banquet, Let It Bleed, Sticky Fingers,* and *Exile on Main Street.*

Miles Davis, 1926-1991 ("My Trumpet")
Pioneered styles that shaped the course of jazz and greatly influenced today's rap and hip-hop movements. He is credited with ushering in what is known as the cool jazz movement in 1949, and fusion (influenced by Sly Stone and Jimi Hendrix) in the late 60s and early 70s. Davis's back-to-the-audience performing style added mystery to his already legendary persona. His music, still as important as ever, continues to influence musicians and fans alike. Suggested listening: *Birth of the Cool, Miles Ahead, Porgy and Bess, Sketches of Spain, Kind of Blue, Milestones,* and *Bitches Brew.*

Charlie "Bird" Parker, 1920-1955 ("Jazz Bath")
Revolutionized jazz by introducing new harmonic and rhythmic possibilities, creating a new style called bebop. Bird took the alto sax and jazz to a whole other level by incorporating more complex improvisations, transforming old standards into something brand new. Along with Dizzy Gillespie, drummers Kenny Clarke and Max Roach, and pianist Thelonius Monk, a new music was born. The musical (r)evolution of bebop spawned some of the world's finest jazz musicians and is still performed and studied worldwide. Suggested listening: *Bird: The Complete Charlie Parker on Verve* and *Jumpin' at the Roost 1948-1949.*

John Coltrane, 1926-1967 ("Jazz Bath")
Known to many as just "Trane," Coltrane's genius pioneered the next evolution in jazz—hard bop. In August of 1959, Coltrane recorded *Giant Steps,* one of the greatest jazz albums of all time. This masterpiece is what Trane is best known for, but it was just the beginning. Joining forces with pianist McCoy Tyner, bassist Jimmy Garrison, and drummer Elvin Jones, Trane created another movement in jazz, known as avant-garde.

Avant-garde predated fusion and, like the music of Jimi Hendrix, reflected the politics and social consciousness of the time. Suggested listening: *Giant Steps, A Love Supreme, My Favorite Things,* and *Interstellar Space.*

Mahalia Jackson, 1911-1972 ("Gospel")
One of the most influential singers in gospel music. Raised Baptist in New Orleans, she learned much musically from the church and was heavily influenced by the great Bessie Smith. Jackson became an ambassador for gospel music, singing all over the world. She performed at an inaugural ball for President John F. Kennedy in 1960, and at many civil-rights rallies held by Dr. Martin Luther King Jr. She sang with vocal ease and a spiritual fervor that still inspires today. Suggested listening: *Gospels, Spirituals & Hymns* (2 CD set, Columbia).

CeCe Winans ("Gospel")
One of the most successful and celebrated contemporary gospel singers in the world. She started her career singing with her brother BeBe and in 1985 released *Lord Lift Us Up,* which went platinum. Her group, the PTL Singers, released five albums, two of which went gold and one platinum. Her first solo album, released in 1995, *Alone in His Presence,* showed her return to her gospel roots. Her 1999 release, *Alabaster Box,* went gold. Winans has received four Grammys, ten Dove Awards, five Stellar Awards, three Image Awards, and one Soul Train Music award. Suggested listening: *Different Lifestyles, Alone in His Presence,* and *Alabaster Box.*

Joni Mitchell, b.1943 ("Today's specials")
Anyone who is even considering getting into songwriting *must* listen to Joni Mitchell. She has influenced most contemporary songwriters, both male and female. From Jewel to Prince, Joni Mitchell is one of the greatest songwriters of all time. A skillful lyricist, Mitchell is also a fine singer and pianist, as well as an extremely

creative guitarist known for her open tunings and unusual chord choices. Mitchell combined elements of folk, jazz, and rock to create her masterpieces. Suggested listening: *Ladies of the Canyon*, *Blue*, and *Court and Spark*.

Giuseppe Verdi, 1813-1901 ("She is")
Post-classical Italian composer who possessed innate gifts for melody and harmony. His compositional skills are said to be unsurpassed by any other opera composer except for Mozart. His works include masterpieces such as *Rigoletto*, *La Traviata*, *Don Carlos*, and *Aida*, which are the cornerstones of most opera houses. Two of his greatest masterpieces came at the end of his life—*Otello* and *Falstaff*.

Giacomo Puccini, 1858-1924 ("She is")
Puccini, like Verdi, was a post-classical Italian composer. Mostly known as a master composer for voice, Puccini was equally adept at harmonic textures and orchestration. Heavily influenced by Verdi and Wagner, Puccini composed some of the world's most famous operas. They include: *La Bohème*, *Tosca*, and *Madama Butterfly*.

Aretha Franklin, Bob Marley, Marvin Gaye, James Brown, Tina Turner. Suggested listening: Anything and everything by these legendary artists!

About the Author

Jaime Adoff is the son of the children's book writer Virginia Hamilton and the poet Arnold Adoff. He grew up in Yellow Springs, Ohio, and received a Bachelor of Music degree from Central State University in Ohio, where he studied drums and percussion. Moving to New York City in 1990, he attended the Manhattan School of Music and studied drums and voice. Adoff then went on to pursue a career in songwriting and fronted his own rock band for eight years. He released two CDs of his own material and performed extensively in New York City and throughout the Northeast.

In 1998 Adoff turned to writing children's and young-adult books. *The Song Shoots Out of My Mouth* is his first published work. Adoff credits his parents for showing him the creative process up close, instilling in him a sense that creating was as ordinary as an everyday job. "It was like magic. They would go into their offices to work, entering with nothing, and come out hours later with pages of writing. That left a lasting impression on me."

About the Illustrator

Martin French says, "Art and music intersect on a daily basis in my life as I carry out my work as an artist and mentor my ten-year-old son's own creative journey—playing jazz guitar and violin."

Mr. French graduated from the Art Center College of Design in Pasadena and went on to work as a designer and art director for Atari and Microsoft before opening his own illustration studio in 1996. His art has won numerous awards, including a 1999 Gold Medal from the Society of Illustrators. This is his first book for young people. He lives in the Pacific Northwest with his wife and two children.